PETS' GUIDES

Giggle's Guide to
Caring for Your Gerbils

Isabel Thomas

Raintree is an imprint of Capstone Global
Library Limited, a company incorporated
in England and Wales having its registered
office at 7 Pilgrim Street, London, EC4V 6LB –
Registered company
number: 6695582

www.raintreepublishers.co.uk
myorders@raintreepublishers.co.uk

Text © Capstone Global Library Limited 2015
First published in hardback in 2014
The moral rights of the proprietor have
been asserted.

Edited by James Benefield and Brynn Baker
Designed by Cynthia Akiyoshi
Picture research by Tracy Cummins
Production by Victoria Fitzgerald
Originated by Capstone Global Library Limited
Printed and bound in China by RR Donnelley
Asia

ISBN 978-1-406-28176-7

18 17 16 15 14
10 9 8 7 6 5 4 3 2 1

British Library Cataloguing in Publication Data
A full catalogue record for this book is
available from the British Library.

Acknowledgements
We would like to thank the following for
permission to reproduce photographs: Alamy: ©
Arco Images GmbH, front cover, © Les Gibbon,
9; Capstone Library: Karon Dubke, 6, 11, 12,
17, 21, 23, 25, 26; Getty Images: Julie Persons
Photography, 5; Glow Images: ARCO/Steimer,
14; Photoshot: Richard Hutchings, 18; Design
Elements Shutterstock: iBird, Picsfive, R-studio.

We would like to thank Jackie Roswell for her
assistance in the preparation of this book.

Contents

Some words are shown in bold, **like this**. You can find out what they mean by looking in the glossary.

Do you want pet gerbils?

Tee hee! I'm Giggle and this book is all about gerbils like me. Gerbils are **rodents**, and we make great pets. You'll love watching us dig and explore our amazing underground tunnels.

Before getting pet gerbils, be sure you can look after us properly. We'll need food, water and a clean place to live. Plus, we need company, safe toys to play with and **vet** care if we get sick or injured. In return, you'll get some new friends!

Choosing your gerbils

If you're ready to care for gerbils, why not adopt your new pets from an **animal shelter** or **rescue centre**! You can also buy gerbils from pet shops or a good **breeder**.

To find healthy gerbils, look for clean, smooth fur, and bright eyes. Healthy gerbils are always busy, and interested in everything. Wow, what's going on over there?

Company

You will need to adopt or buy at least two gerbils. I get very lonely when I'm on my own. I need gerbil friends to play with all the time. Not just any gerbils though!

Choose a group of boy gerbils or a group of girl gerbils. If you see two gerbils rubbing noses or **grooming** each other, you know they are good friends.

Getting ready

Are you ready to go house-hunting? Your new pet would love a **gerbilarium** to come home to. Find one with lots of space and places to hide. Fill it with stuff to dig through. Gerbils love digging deep burrows.

Gerbil at work

Giggle's gerbil shopping list:

- a large gerbilarium
- nesting material (such as shredded paper)
- bedding material (such as dust-free wood shavings)
- a water bottle
- things to play with (no plastic please!)
- a rough stone
- a **gnawing** block

Welcome home

Moving can be scary, especially for gerbils. Put my gerbilarium in a quiet place. My ears are small but sensitive, and I can hear lots of noises that you can't hear. The sound of televisions, computers, vacuum cleaners and running water all hurt my ears.

Draughts, damp places, bright sunlight and radiators are also bad for gerbils. Worst of all are other animals! Even the smell of a cat or dog makes me s-s-s-scared.

Pick me up

Thank you for working hard to make my perfect home. At first I'll feel very shy and spend lots of time hiding. Don't worry, I'll be ready to make friends soon.

Here's how to get gerbils used to being stroked and held.

🐾 Be quiet and slow, so I'm not scared.

🐾 Gently cup my body with both hands.

🐾 Offer me treats, and let me sniff your hands.

🐾 Never pick me up by my tail.

🐾 Sit down, so I won't get hurt if I wriggle out of your hands.

Playtime

Once I'm used to you, handle me every day. Gerbils are awake during the day, and we love company. Make sure we can still play, run and dig when you're not here. You can buy special gerbil toys and running wheels from pet shops.

Try making your own gerbil adventure playground. Build tunnels out of cardboard tubes, wood or hay. Let us play outside the gerbilarium, too, but make the room hard to escape. Watch us carefully in case we get into trouble!

Feeding time

All that fun makes me hungry. Special gerbil food has everything we need to stay healthy. Try scattering the food over our bedding. It's great fun searching for it, and it will stop us from fighting over one dish.

Give me fresh vegetables to nibble every day.
Fruit and seeds are yummy, but save them for
special treats. There are some foods that we
can't eat – check the list on page 29.

Cleaning my home

I need a clean home to stay healthy. Check my gerbilarium every day, and throw away any wet or dirty bedding. Look for piles of leftover food that I've hidden for later! **Stale** food could give me a tummy ache.

Wash out the whole gerbilarium every week. Save some of the dry bedding and nesting material. You can mix it with our new bedding to make sure our gerbilarium still smells like home.

Grooming and gnawing

A daily bath keeps my **coat** clean, but I don't need water. Gerbils bathe in sand! Fill a shallow tray with **chinchilla sand** and let me roll around. When I've finished, you can clean the sand by sifting it, and I'll use it again next time.

I'm a rodent, so my teeth and claws never stop growing. Remember the rough stone and gnawing block on my shopping list? Walking over the stone and chewing on the block keeps my claws and teeth trim.

Visiting the vet

Gerbils usually live for three to four years. Take me to the vet for a check-up every year. The vet will make sure I'm happy and healthy. I'll also need to see the vet if I seem ill between check-ups.

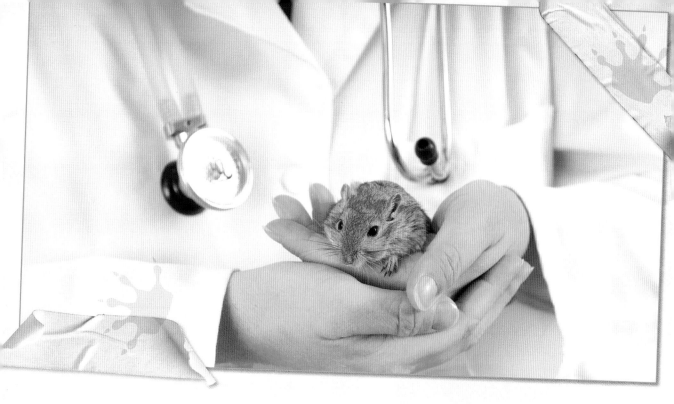

Look out for these signs of a sick gerbil:

- 🐾 I'm eating or drinking more or less than normal
- 🐾 my poo looks wet
- 🐾 the fur on my bottom is dirty
- 🐾 my teeth are getting too long
- 🐾 I do the same thing over and over and am acting confused
- 🐾 there are **fleas** or **lice** on my body

Avoiding change

If you go on holiday, ask a friend or neighbour to visit us every day. Tell them how to keep us happy and healthy. They'll need to fill our food and water, keep our home clean, and watch out for signs of sickness.

If we have to go on a journey, carry us in our gerbilarium. Pack lots of food and water, and use a special cover to make it dark. Travelling is fun for people but not for gerbils. We'd rather stay at home, and hear all about the travelling when you return.

Gerbil facts

- Gerbils have furry feet, which means they can't climb very well.

- Wild gerbils live in deserts and grasslands, in deep underground burrows. This is why they love digging tunnels.

- Giggle is a Mongolian gerbil. These are the type of gerbils usually kept as pets.

- Gerbils are good pets for people who are used to handling small animals. They can be very quick! If you are choosing your first pet, think about getting hamsters or guinea pigs instead.

Giggle's top tips

- Give me toys that are safe to chew, such as branches from apple trees, cardboard tubes and egg boxes.

- Small pieces of carrot, cucumber, broccoli, pumpkin and fennel are good snacks to give me every day.

- Don't give me too many sunflower seeds. I love them, but they are very fatty.

- Gerbils can't eat rhubarb, cabbage, potatoes, onions, uncooked beans, chocolate or sweets. These foods can make us very sick!

Glossary

animal shelter places for animals with no homes

breeder person who helps animals to have babies in an organized way

chinchilla sand special dust-free sand that is safe for pets to dig and bathe in

coat fur or hair that covers an animal

draught cool breeze inside a building, from an open door or window

flea tiny jumping insect that lives on larger animals

gerbilarium special tank for keeping pet gerbils

gnaw bite or chew something again and again

groom clean an animal's fur or skin

lice tiny insects that live on larger animals

rescue centre organization that rescues animals that are lost, injured or not being taken care of properly

rodent type of animal with front teeth that never stop growing, like gerbils

stale no longer fresh and good to eat

vet person trained to care for sick and injured animals

Find out more

Books

Hamster and Gerbil (My New Pet), Jinny Johnson (Franklin Watts, 2013)

Humphrey's World of Pets, Betty G. Birney (Puffin Books, 2013)

Looking After Gerbils (Usborne Pet Guides), Laura Howell (Usborne, 2013)

Websites

www.pdsa.org.uk/pet-health-advice/gerbils
The PDSA website has advice about caring for pet gerbils.

www.rspca.org.uk
The website of the RSPCA (Royal Society for the Prevention of Cruelty to Animals) has information about pet gerbils and how to look after them.

Index